Ben's

Story by Beverley Randell
Illustrated by Genevieve Rees

Mom said,
"Dad is coming home today."

Ben shouted,
"Today! Today!
Dad is coming home today."

Ben went to school.
"My dad is coming home today,"
he said to the teacher.

"My dad is coming home today,"
he said to the boys and girls.

"I'm going to paint my dad," said Ben.

"Where is your dad?"
said the teacher.

"Look," said Ben. "Look down here.
Look at the engines.
Dad takes care of the engines
on the ship."

After school the teacher said,
"Ben – look!
Here comes your dad."

"Hello, Ben," said Dad.
"Dad, Dad!" shouted Ben.

And Ben went home with Dad.